MY BEST BOOK OF
BUGS

Claire Llewellyn

KINGFISHER
KNOW | WONDER
www.kingfisherbooks.com

KINGFISHER
LONDON & NEW YORK

Copyright © Macmillan Publishers International Ltd 2005, 2018
First published 1995 in the United States by Kingfisher
This edition published 2018 by Kingfisher
175 Fifth Ave., New York, NY 10010
Kingfisher is an imprint of Macmillan Children's Books, London
All rights reserved.

Distributed in the U.S. and Canada by Macmillan,
175 Fifth Ave., New York, NY 10010

Library of Congress Cataloging-in-Publication data has been
applied for.

ISBN 978-0-7534-7460-0

Design by Wildpixel Ltd.
Illustrations: Ray Grinaway, Roger Stewart

Kingfisher books are available for special promotions and
premiums. For details contact: Special Markets Department,
Macmillan, 175 Fifth Ave., New York, NY 10010

For more information please visit
www.kingfisherbooks.com

Printed in China
9 8 7 6 5 4 3 2 1
1TR/0618/UNTD/WKT/128MA

Picture credits
The Publisher would like to thank the following for permission to
reproduce their material.
Top = t; Bottom = b; Center = c; Left = l; Right = r
Cover Shutterstock/Maciej Olszewski; Page 1 iStock/lavoview;
2–3, 32 iStock/~UserGI15633745; 2b, 12 iStock/Antagain;
4–5 Shutterstock/fotolistic; 4 Shutterstock/ledyx; 5tl Shutterstock/ Maciej
Olszewski; 5tr Shutterstock/Patrick foto; 5br Shutterstock/dangdrumrong;
6–7 Shutterstock/amfroey; 8–9 iStock/narvikk; 9 Getty/Erich Kuchling;
10 Shutterstock/Pong Wira; 12–13 iStock/temmuzcan; 16–17
Shutterstock/Sura Nualpradid; 18–19 iStock/nutnarin; 19l Shutterstock/
wagtail; 19tr iStock/IMNATURE; 20 Shutterstock/goldenjack;
21t Shutterstock/irin-k; 22–23 iStock/borchee; 22bl Shutterstock/Hanka
Steidle; 22tr iStock/NexTser; 23tl iStock/Michael Burrell; 23cl iStock/
stanley45; 23c iStock/fmajor; 23bl iStock/liouzojan; 24tl Shutterstock/
Anthony Paz; 25br inset Shutterstock/Karlosevitch; 26–27 all elements
Shutterstock; 26bl Alamy/Minden Pictures; 26br Shutterstock/Valerijs
Vahrusevs; 26c Shutterstock/Zadiraka Evgenii; 27tl Shutterstock/Michal
Hykel; 27tr Shutterstock/aslutsky; 27cr Shutterstock/Dirk Ercken;
28–29 background Shutterstock/RENATOK; 28–29 iStock/vnlit;
30–31 background Shutterstock/BlackRabbit3; 30r iStock/Jeremy_Hogan;
31t iStock/TommyIX; 31c iStock/Vac1.

CONTENTS

A SMALL WORLD

Can you imagine what it's like to be very, very tiny? Millions of creatures are no bigger than your fingernail. For them, the grass is as thick as a forest and a flowering plant is as tall as a tree!

Being small might sound scary, but it can be useful. Tiny bugs can hide anywhere—under a leaf, inside a nut, or deep in an animal's fur. There, they are safe from birds, frogs, and other sharp-eyed animals that feed on them.

Hiding places

Bugs live all around us, yet most of the time we don't even know that they are there. Look for them in the places where they like to hide—under a stone, inside a flowerpot, or in the crack of a wall.

A BIG COLLECTION

There are millions of different bugs and spiders all over the world. In fact, there are more bugs in the world than any other type of animal. Scientists have sorted them into groups. Each group contains animals with the same type of body.

Bugs

Many bugs look very different from one another, but they all have three pairs of legs and three parts to their body—the head, thorax, and abdomen. All bugs and spiders have a hard casing on the outside of their body called an exoskeleton. This protects an animal's soft insides, just like a strong suit of armor. Many bugs also have wings, and most have long feelers called antennae.

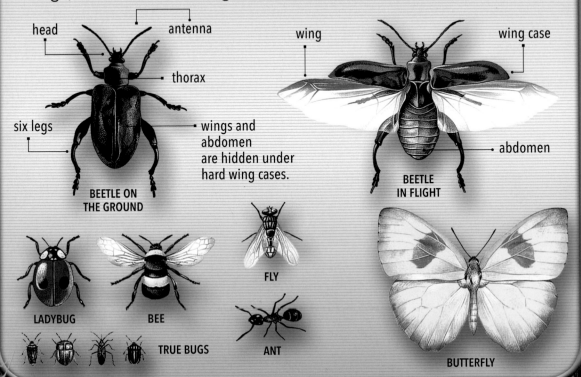

head

antenna

thorax

six legs

wings and abdomen are hidden under hard wing cases.

BEETLE ON THE GROUND

wing

wing case

abdomen

BEETLE IN FLIGHT

LADYBUG

BEE

FLY

TRUE BUGS

ANT

BUTTERFLY

Arachnids

Spiders have two parts to their body—the head and thorax at the front and the abdomen at the back. Spiders have four pairs of legs, one more pair than bugs.

Other creepy-crawlies

Centipedes and millipedes have a long, wriggly body made up of segments. Centipedes have one pair of legs on each segment; millipedes have two.

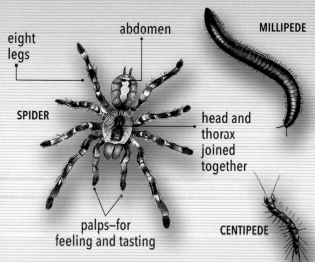

eight legs

abdomen

MILLIPEDE

SPIDER

head and thorax joined together

palps–for feeling and tasting

CENTIPEDE

SNAIL

Snails and slugs don't have legs. They crawl along on their soft belly. Snails live inside a hard shell. Slugs survive without a shell.

Scorpions, mites, and ticks are closely related to spiders. Scorpions have two parts to their body; mites and ticks have one. Like spiders, they each have four pairs of legs.

SCORPION

SOIL MITE

RED VELVET MITE

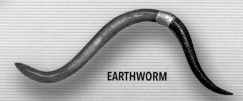

EARTHWORM

Earthworms have a long, soft body that is covered with tiny bristles. They don't have a skeleton or shell to protect them. They live in soft, damp soil under the ground.

SPINNING SPIDERS

Spiders are amazing creatures. They can make a silk that is stronger than steel and weave it into beautiful, lacy webs. The webs are important because many spiders have poor eyesight and their sticky traps help them catch their food. When an insect flies into the web, the spider feels it instantly through the vibrations and rushes over for the kill.

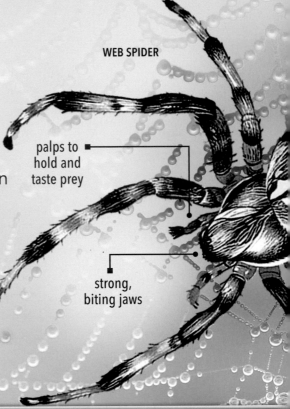

WEB SPIDER

palps to hold and taste prey

strong, biting jaws

Sheet-web spider

A sheet-web spider spins a flat web with crisscrossing threads above it. Small bugs crash into the threads and fall on the web below.

Net-casting spider

A net-casting spider hangs head down and holds its silk web in its front legs. It throws the web, like a net, to trap its prey.

Water spider

A water spider lives in a bell-shaped web under the surface of the water. It dashes out and seizes tiny creatures as they paddle by.

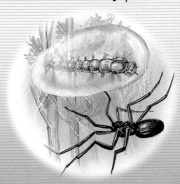

Silk comes out through tiny tubes called spinnerets.

delicate hairs on legs

When a struggling bug is caught in its web, the spider injects it with venom and wraps it up tightly in silk. The venom kills the bug and turns it into a runny food that the spider sucks up like a drink.

Spinning a web

Many spiders build a new web every day. Garden spiders spin round webs. It usually takes them around an hour to make one.

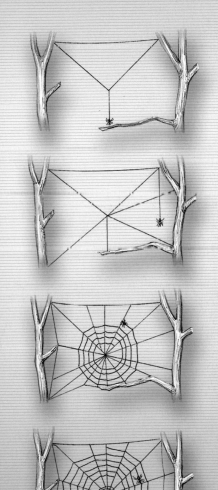

HUNTING SPIDERS

Hunting spiders don't use webs. Instead, they chase, ambush, or leap on their prey. They have sharp eyes to help them spot their prey and strong legs to help them catch it. Their jaws are good for biting. Some spiders also use their jaws to dig burrows, where they hide and lie in wait.

Trapdoor spider

A trapdoor spider builds an underground burrow by shoveling away the soil with its jaws. Then it lines the burrow with silk, covers it with a lid, and camouflages it with twigs and grass. The lid keeps out enemies and the rain. At dusk, the trapdoor spider lifts the lid of its burrow and waits. As soon as a creature passes by, the spider leaps out, stuns it with venom, and drags it back into its burrow to eat.

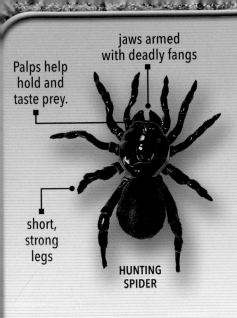

Palps help hold and taste prey.

jaws armed with deadly fangs

short, strong legs

HUNTING SPIDER

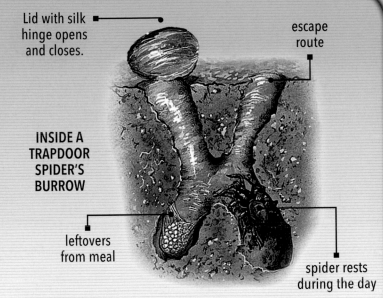

Lid with silk hinge opens and closes.

escape route

INSIDE A TRAPDOOR SPIDER'S BURROW

leftovers from meal

spider rests during the day

Wandering spider

The wandering spider doesn't have a home. It is always on the move, hunting for a tasty cockroach or caterpillar.

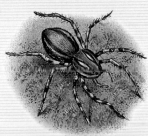

Jumping spider

The sharp-eyed jumping spider stalks its prey like a cat and then suddenly pounces for the kill.

Bolas spider

The bolas spider catches bugs with a sticky line of silk that it swings around like a lasso.

Spitting spider

The spitting spider traps bugs with a sticky gum fired through its fangs.

11

BUZZING BEES

Honeybees are busy all summer long. They fly from flower to flower, feeding on the sweet nectar inside. There are many different types of bee. Most live on their own, either in a burrow or a hollow stem. But honeybees live with thousands of others in a huge group called a colony. A colony works as a team. Together, the bees build a nest, find food, fight their enemies, and take care of their young.

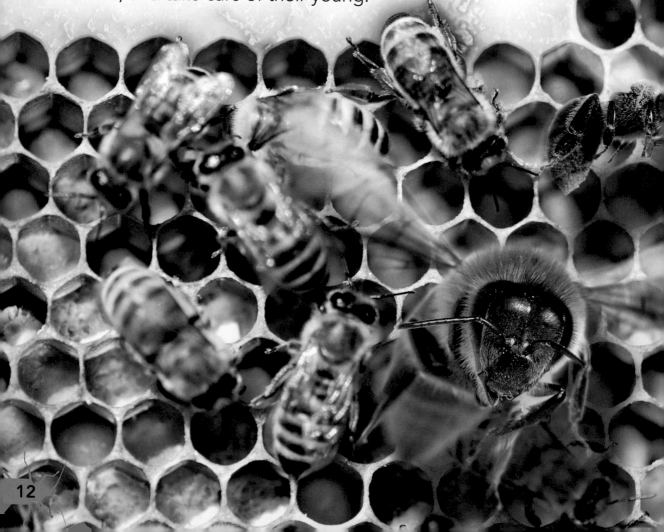

WASP

BEE

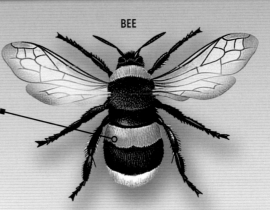

Bold stripes warn that these animals sting.

A wasps' nest

Wasps live in colonies, too. Every year, they build a new nest out of thin sheets of paper. They make the paper by chewing tiny pieces of wood and mixing it with their saliva. The nest has a small doorway that is always guarded. The wasps keep their eggs and young safe inside.

A bees' nest

Honeybees build their nest in a cave or a hollow tree. Bees make a waxy material that they shape into long slabs called honeycomb. A bees' nest is strong and may last 50 years or more.

13

THE HONEYBEE'S YEAR

All honeybees start as an egg, and grow from larva to pupa into a fully grown bee. Every bee has a job to do, and each job is important to the wellbeing of the nest.

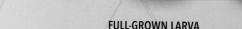

EGG

YOUNG LARVA

FULL-GROWN LARVA

PUPA

WORKER

DRONE

QUEEN

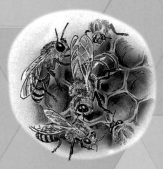

1. In a honeybees' nest, most of the bees are females, called workers. A few of the bees are males, called drones. One of the bees is a queen.

2. When she is young, the queen bee mates with the drones. Soon afterward, she begins to lay thousands of eggs. She lays each egg in its own little pocket, or cell, in the honeycomb.

3. After three days, the eggs hatch into wriggly grubs called larvae. The worker bees feed the larvae with nectar and pollen from flowers.

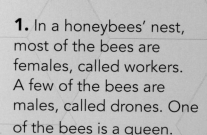

14

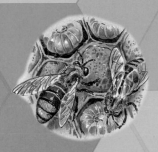  

4. After a few days, the larvae are fully grown, and the workers seal their cells with wax. Inside, each larva changes into a pupa, which then becomes a bee.

5. The new bees start work as soon as they hatch. They clean the nest, feed the queen, and take care of the next batch of eggs.

6. As they grow older, the young bees start to make wax and build new slabs of honeycomb to hold extra food supplies for the winter.

7. During the summer, the workers leave the nest to gather food. They suck sugary nectar from flowers with their long tongue.

8. Pollen is a yellow dust made by flowers. As they eat, the bees comb pollen onto their back legs and carry it back to the nest.

9. Inside the nest, the nectar is turned into honey and is stored in the cells. The pollen is stored there, too, in layers.

 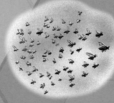 

10. When a bee finds a new source of food, it returns to the nest and does a special dance to tell the other bees where they can find it, too.

11. If a bees' nest gets too crowded, the old queen flies off with a swarm of workers to start a new nest. A larva in the old nest grows into a new queen.

12. Honeybees rest in the winter, feeding on their honey supply and staying warm. In the spring, they fly off in search of more nectar.

HARD-WORKING ANTS

Ants make their nest under large stones or plants. Each nest contains hundreds of ants. One of them, the queen, lays all the eggs. The others are workers. They do different jobs around the nest, such as feeding the larvae or gathering food. Ants eat all types of plants and animals. When they find food, they mark a trail back to the nest with a powerful scent, which the other ants quickly follow.

QUEEN

WORKER

Weaver ants

Weaver ants work as a team to build their nest. Some of the ants hold leaves together. Others bind the edges of the leaves together with sticky, silky thread made by their larvae.

The queen ant

A queen ant has wings at first, but pulls them out after she flies off to mate with a male. She spends the rest of her life laying hundreds of eggs.

Honeypot ants

Honeypot ants use some of their workers as jars. When flowers are plentiful, they fill the workers with nectar. They "milk" these ant-jars when food is harder to find.

An ants' nest

There are many different rooms inside an ants' nest. Some are nurseries for the eggs, larvae, and pupae. Others are used to store food or garbage. Worker ants are always busy. Some take care of the queen and nurseries. Others guard the entrance to the nest, attack intruders, and search for food. Ants tap one another with their antennae to pass information.

BUSY BEETLES

All types of beetles crawl over the woodland floor, busily looking for food. Some munch on plants. Others are hunters that kill and eat other creatures or nibble on their rotting remains. Beetles are small but very important. As they crawl and eat their way through the leaves, they mix dead plants and animals into the soil. This nourishes the soil and helps new plants grow. Many other bugs live in woodlands, too, because there is plenty of food.

A beetle's bite

Many beetles have powerful jaws for grabbing, biting, and chewing their prey. This stag beetle is a male. Its huge jaws look like horns or antlers. It uses them to fight other males.

STAG
BEETLE

ALL TYPES OF BEETLES

Beetles are the largest group of animals in the world. There are more than 300,000 different types. Most beetles have a hard, tough exoskeleton that protects them from their enemies. Some beetles are also armed with strong jaws or sharp spines.

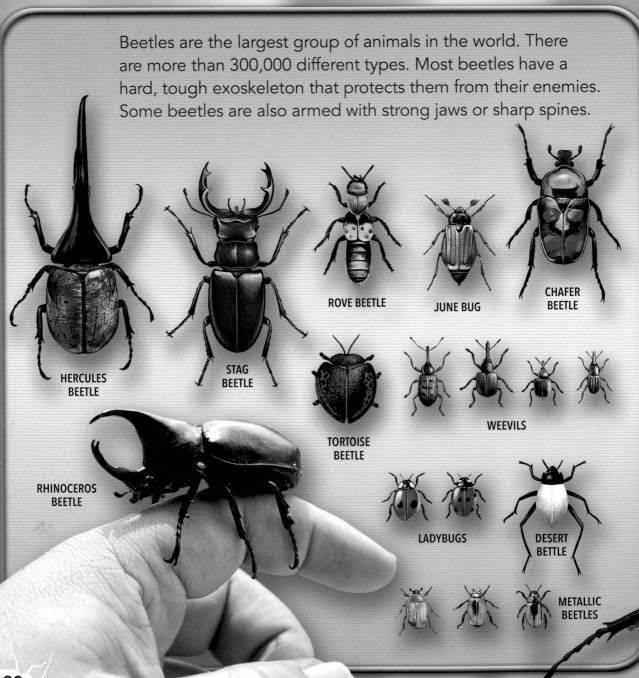

ROVE BEETLE

JUNE BUG

CHAFER BEETLE

HERCULES BEETLE

STAG BEETLE

TORTOISE BEETLE

WEEVILS

RHINOCEROS BEETLE

LADYBUGS

DESERT BETTLE

METALLIC BEETLES

Many beetles are brightly colored to warn hungry enemies that they taste bad. A few are actually poisonous. Some beetles have stripes, like a wasp. This helps keep enemies away– even though these beetles cannot sting!

Burying beetles
Burying beetles bury dead animals and lay their eggs on top. Their tiny larvae then have plenty to eat.

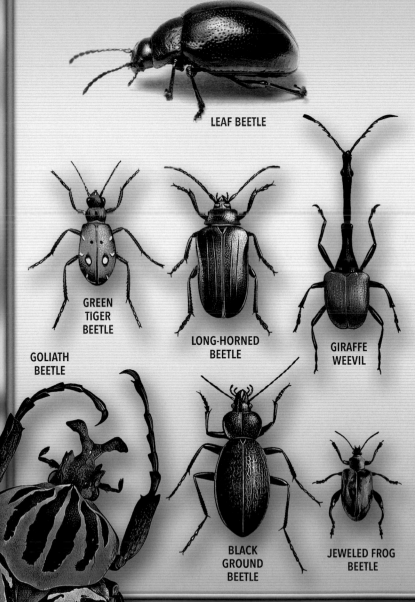

LEAF BEETLE

GREEN TIGER BEETLE

LONG-HORNED BEETLE

GIRAFFE WEEVIL

GOLIATH BEETLE

BLACK GROUND BEETLE

JEWELED FROG BEETLE

Dung beetles
Dung beetles lay their eggs inside balls of animal dung, which they then bury under the ground.

Nut weevils
Nut weevils drill holes in nuts and lay their eggs inside. The larvae eat the nuts from the inside out.

BUTTERFLIES AND MOTHS

BLUE GLASSY TIGER
BUTTERFLY

Beautiful butterflies flutter through the air, flashing their
brightly colored wings. Butterflies are active during the day.
They feed on flowers, sucking up nectar with their long, curly
tongue. Moths are usually active at night. In the daytime,
many moths rest on a tree's trunk or branches. Their
dull brown markings match a tree's speckled bark.
This camouflage makes the moths hard to see.

SWALLOWTAIL

clubbed antennae

feathered antennae

plump body

delicate body

ORANGE-BARRED SULFUR BUTTERFLY

LEOPARD MOTH

MONARCH BUTTERFLY

Butterfly or moth?

Butterflies are usually brighter than moths and have a more delicate body. A butterfly's antennae are clubbed at the tip. A moth's are usually feathery.

BLUE MORPHO BUTTERFLY

GREEN BIRDWING BUTTERFLY

EGG TO BUTTERFLY

Like many bugs, butterflies change completely as they grow. This change is called metamorphosis.

1. Red admiral butterfly lays egg on leaf.

2. Caterpillar hatches from egg.

3. Caterpillar changes into pupa.

4. Butterfly dries wings in the air.

There are around 150,000 types of butterfly and moth, and they and their caterpillars come in all sorts of colors and sizes. The Atlas moth is as big as a dinner plate. The Western pygmy blue butterfly is not much wider than your thumb.

LUNA MOTH

MADAGASCAN SUNSET MOTH

88 BUTTERFLY

CAIRN'S BIRDWING BUTTERFLY AND CATERPILLAR

GYPSY MOTH

ORANGE-TIP BUTTERFLY

COMMON BLUE BUTTERFLY AND CATERPILLAR

SMOOTH EMERALD MOTH

RED ADMIRAL BUTTERFLY

CABBAGE WHITE BUTTERFLY

HORNET BUTTERFLY

ATLAS MOTH

SWALLOW TAIL BUTTERFLY AND CATEPILLAR

COMMA BUTTERFLY AND CATERPILLAR

Bright wings

The wings of butterflies and moths are covered with tiny scales that shimmer in the light. Some of them are brightly colored. Others have bold patterns or scary eyespots. When a butterfly or moth flashes its wings at its enemies, it confuses them and gives it time to escape.

POND LIFE

Life in a pond is not as peaceful as it seems. Huge dragonflies dart noisily through the air, snatching at flies. Dainty damselflies flash like jewels in the sun as they snap at gnats and midges. Other hunters live in the water itself and pounce on anything that moves. Not every small creature leaves the pond. Some, like water scorpions and spiders, spend their entire life under the water.

NYMPH

EGG

26

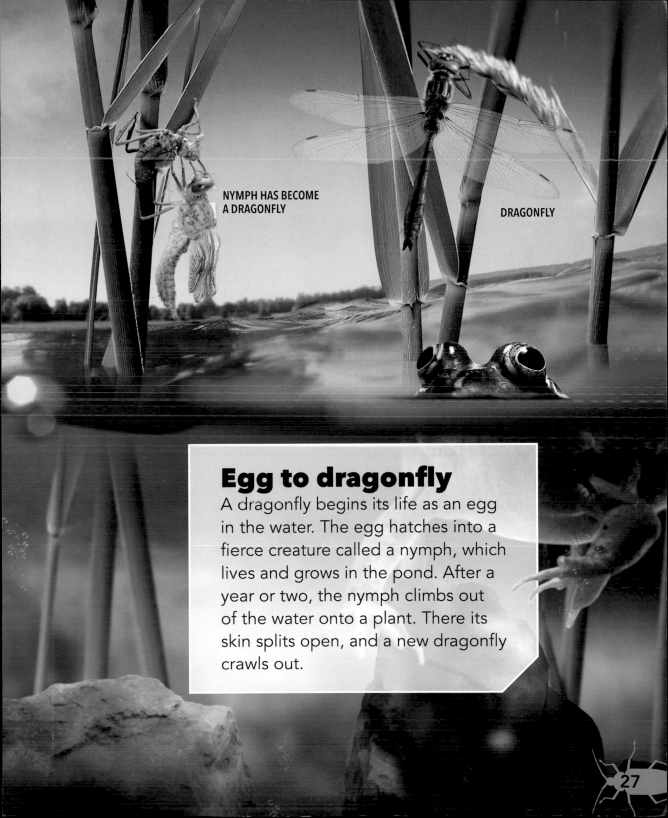

NYMPH HAS BECOME
A DRAGONFLY

DRAGONFLY

Egg to dragonfly

A dragonfly begins its life as an egg
in the water. The egg hatches into a
fierce creature called a nymph, which
lives and grows in the pond. After a
year or two, the nymph climbs out
of the water onto a plant. There its
skin splits open, and a new dragonfly
crawls out.

DARTING DRAGONFLIES

A dragonfly is a powerful flier. It has two pairs of wings, and each pair works on its own. This helps the dragonfly twist, turn, change its speed, or hover over the water.

Catching a meal

1. A dragonfly nymph lurks deep in the pond, camouflaged by its muddy colors. Suddenly a tadpole swims past.

2. Quickly, the nymph shoots out a pair of sharp, hooked jaws and grabs its prey.

3. The nymph's deadly jaws slide back to its mouth, and the hunter feeds on its catch.

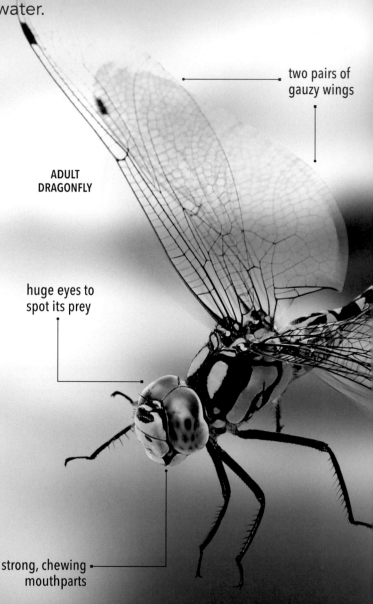

two pairs of gauzy wings

ADULT DRAGONFLY

huge eyes to spot its prey

strong, chewing mouthparts

DAMSELFLY NYMPH

ADULT DAMSELFLY

Living on water

All animals need oxygen. Some pond creatures get oxygen from the water. Others get it from the air.

Like dragonflies, damselflies and caddis flies lay their eggs in ponds. A damselfly egg hatches into a nymph. A caddis fly egg hatches into a larva.

CADDIS FLY LARVA

A damselfly nymph has three gills on its tail, which soak up oxygen in water.

A water scorpion floats to the surface of the water and takes in air through a tube.

ADULT CADDIS FLY

A diving beetle collects air bubbles and stores them under its wings.

29

OUT AT NIGHT

Summer nights are alive with all types of bug. Crickets chirp, mosquitoes hum, and tiny fireflies flash in the dark. This is their way of talking to one another. Night is a good time for some bugs because the air is cool and many of their enemies are asleep. Through the hours of darkness, these tiny creatures feed, hunt, and look for a mate. At dawn they hide, and the bees, butterflies, and other sun-loving creatures return with the warmth and light.

GLOSSARY

abdomen The back part of a bug's body. Inside the abdomen is the heart and the various parts that break down food and help a creature produce its young.

antenna (plural antennae) One of a pair of feelers that pick up scents and tastes in the air and help an animal feel its way around.

bug (or insect) An animal with three parts to its body and three pairs of jointed legs.

camouflage The colors and markings on an animal that help it blend in with its surroundings and make it difficult to see.

colony A large group of animals that live together. Honeybees live in a colony, as do ants.

drone A male honeybee, whose only job is to mate with the queen.

exoskeleton The hard casing on the outside of the body of most bugs.

fang The clawlike part of a spider's jaws that it uses to stick into an animal and inject venom.

gill The part of an animal's body that allows it to breathe under the water. The gills soak up oxygen that has dissolved in the water. The nymphs of water bugs, such as damselflies, have gills.

grub Another name for the legless larva of an insect.

larva (plural larvae) The young stage of an insect after it hatches from an egg, which looks very different from an adult. A larva has to pass through a pupa stage before it becomes an adult bug.

metamorphosis The change from a young bug into an adult bug—for example, from a caterpillar to a butterfly.

nectar The sugary juice inside flowers that attracts bugs and other small animals. Bees use nectar to make honey.

nymph The young stage of a bug, such as a grasshopper or a dragonfly, that changes gradually into an adult without passing through a pupa stage.

oxygen A gas that all animals need to breathe in order to survive. Oxygen is one of the gases found in the air and water.

palp One of a pair of feelers near the jaws of a spider or a bug that feel and taste its food.

pollen The yellow dustlike powder made by flowers. When bugs carry it to the same type of flowers, they can make seeds.

pupa (plural pupae) The stage in a bug's life when it changes from a larva to an adult. In butterflies and moths, the pupa is called the chrysalis.

thorax The middle part of a bug's body, in between the head and the abdomen. A bug's wings and legs are attached to the thorax.

true bug A group of bugs with a long, sharp feeding tube, which they use to pierce animals or plants and suck out their juices.

INDEX